WITHOUT FEAR OF SUCCESS

"THE SUCCESS OF ANOTHER IS ALSO YOUR SUCCESS"

Adriana Calabria

SUCCESS AS A RESULT OF FAITH IN GOD

COMMENTS
Without fear of success

The favor and hand of God are essential to achieve success in our path and in that of those around us.

You will find inspiration in this book, which will encourage you to move forward and understand how relationships are very valid and important to achieve lasting success.

You will see the story of young Joseph who, through relationships, positioned himself "without fear of success" in the office that gave him all the authority and domain for a specific task.

Dr. Adriana Calabria, writer of "Without Fear of Success" is a living example of someone who enjoys the guidance and hand of the Lord over her life, family, and ministry, and with spiritual authority, she tells us how we can advance in life by seeking to please God in the eternal calling.

How important it is to be able to measure success in helping others achieve their most desired dreams, that is to serve, when we serve God we have to keep in mind that we serve people.

I encourage you to dare to delve into the reading and knowledge expressed in the pages of this powerful book, where there is no room for doubt or turning back.

I can say that with faith in God, you will be able to achieve what you set out to do, "Without Fear of Success".

Go ahead, the best is just a few steps ahead!

Dr. Osvaldo Diaz
Apostle - Founding President of CODM
Durham, NC USA.

Only guided and inspired by God can we achieve lasting, progressive, and transcendental success. True success is not just about oneself, but about knowing that we need others to achieve it and that we should help others achieve it, and be happy for their success.

That is one of the wise messages of this powerful book, *Without Fear of Success*. Dr. Adriana Calabria reveals to us with great success this universal "recipe" that she professes for her ministerial and personal success. Why "without fear"? Because if we know that God promises to be with us always and fight our battles, we do not have to be afraid of the path that leads to success or of success itself.

I invite you to read and learn the valuable and specific lessons contained in this book. They will lead you to success with a firm faith in God.
Be blessed!

Pastor Ofelia Perez, AWA
President, Power Lion Books
Davidson, NC

Unless otherwise indicated, all Scripture quotations have been taken from The Holy Bible, English Standard Version® (ESV®) © 2001 by Crossway, a publishing ministry of Good News Publishers. All rights reserved. Scripture quotations marked (CEV) are from the Contemporary English Version Copyright © 1991, 1992, 1995 by American Bible Society. Used by Permission. Scripture quotations marked TPT are from The Passion Translation®. Copyright © 2017, 2018, 2020 by Passion & Fire Ministries, Inc. Used by permission. All rights reserved. ThePassionTranslation.com.

Edited by: Michelle Juárez

WITHOUT FEAR OF SUCCESS

"The success of others is also your success"

ISBN: 979-8-9899399-1-6

© 2024 by Adriana Calabria

Adriana Calabria Publishing, LLC

Printed in the United States of America

No part of this publication may be reproduced or transmitted in any form or by any electronic or mechanical means; including photocopying, recording, or by any storage and retrieval system, without the prior written permission of the author.

DEDICATION

Agustín Díaz, my son, this book is for you. You were born to succeed, you are not afraid of success.

PREFACE

This book is for those who want to achieve lasting success, God's way.

With so many studies on the subject, this book will revolutionize your concepts, because success by God's way is different from success by man's way.

Spiritual leadership differs greatly from the ideas that the world has, and those of us who are spiritual have a greater responsibility because we will be accountable to God for each of our actions, including the way we lead and encourage others to achieve their goals.

It is wonderful to see when God, who does everything differently from how we believe and understand, raises the smallest and most humble, the one we least imagined, whom we helped achieve it.

Praying for each person that God allows us to lead and influence is very important because it gives us the correct perspective to succeed. That's what it's all about, enjoying your successes and those of others. You succeed when you help others succeed.

I read something that made me laugh, but it is true: some people have a buffet-type faith, that is, they take from the Word of God what they like, although they do not take into account its commandments, which are not burdensome, rather they provide benefits, long life, and prosperity.

So, to help others succeed, we must guide them to the

truth of God, in addition to seeking the treasure that each person carries within. In some, said treasure is buried or locked with a padlock because the enemy wants to prevent us from discovering it since it is a weapon that can defeat him.

Therefore, discovering these treasures, bringing those potentialities to light and activating them will require a lot of effort, but it will be worth it. Nothing is more satisfying than helping people have real experiences with success. Do you know what's truly wonderful? That those people you helped will be with you for the rest of your life.

A big part of my success is knowing how many benefits others have achieved by providing them with the knowledge of God's Word. When one dedicates oneself to what he or she loves, the predominant gift that God deposited takes us out of pigeonholing and routine to lead us toward true success. Believe it!

CONTENT

1. Success God's Way — 19
2. Success is a process — 25
3. Be unconditional help — 29
4. Success is built with words — 33
5. Humility is needed — 37
6. Loyalty VS. Disloyalty — 41
7. The spirit of independence — 47
8. Prophesy life — 51
9. Stubbornness VS. Wisdom — 55
10. Shame or bravery — 59
11. Power… what for? — 63
12. The hand of God over my life — 67
13. Your heart's desire — 71
14. Enjoying these times is decisive — 75
15. The strong and the weak — 79
16. Ask for justice — 83
17. It will be established unto you — 87

18.	Successful conclusion	91
19.	Staying on top	95
20.	Desperate seeking produces unlimited protection	99
21.	God is always working a new genesis	103
22.	What was lost	107
23.	True success is being a part of His kingdom	111
24.	Passion for your eternal calling	115
25.	When abundance exceeds you	119

| Without fear of success | 123 |
| Final words | 127 |

SUCCESS GOD'S WAY

CHAPTER 1

Fear is positive when it gives rise to courage, it is like that opponent that makes you work harder to improve yourself.

There is a big difference between success according to the world and success according to God's parameters. Sadly, Christians are not exempt from the disease of success according to the world. But much more transcendent is the success by the hand of God. In all areas of our lives, we want to achieve success. This is a reality in work, finances, business, marriage, children, friendships, etc.

Many claim to want success, but they are really afraid of it. Something strange, right? But even if you are afraid, you have to try. I'm sorry to say, but not everything we do will be successful, certain situations need to occur in our lives so that the courage that will emerge in us will strengthen us on the path to success.

For example, fear is positive when it gives rise to courage; It is like that opponent or competitor that pressures us to work harder to improve ourselves. Commonly, we think of fear as something negative, but if through the work of God courage grows in us, we draw strength from God, no more and no less. Then, only there, we are stronger than our trials or difficulties.

And it is through people, through strategic relationships, that we achieve success. Success does not come alone, it comes together with people who help us achieve it. All disappointments come from people who hurt us. That is why when you never want to see a person again, lend them money. And know that God allows us to come to the place of failure to break our pride. Therefore, we must have humility and know that we are not alone.

The Word of God says in 1 John 4:18 (ESV): *There is no fear in love, but perfect love casts out fear…*

Precisely by receiving the powerful love of God, we drive away hatred, resentment, and fear and it becomes easier for us to love others. The path to success is for someone to come into your life and extend a hand to fulfill your assignment. That happened to Joseph in the biblical story when he met Pharaoh's baker in prison. Then, that baker remembered Joseph after two years and thus began the new life of this son of Jacob as he interpreted Pharaoh's dreams and rose to power.

Joseph went from poverty to riches in one day. But his support was the Spirit of God that lived in him. Everything we do influenced and directed by the Spirit of God will turn out well for us. True success, above all things, is doing the will of God and in this way being a person with true influence for the benefit of those around us.

This is captured in what **apostle Paul wrote in 1 Corinthians 3:18-19 (ESV):** *Let no one deceive himself. If anyone among you thinks that he is wise in this age, let him become a fool that he may become wise. For the wisdom of this world is folly with God. For it is written, "He catches the wise in their craftiness,"*

It is impossible to achieve something if you tell yourself: *"I am too ignorant"* or *"I am too slow"* when in reality you must feed your spirit with positive words and thoughts. Although success does not come alone, it comes along with people who help us achieve it, there will be times in your life when you will have to learn to walk alone.

Not everyone who begins with you will end by your side.

When I was a child, our family had a dog named Buki. He was so good that his great size did not match his nobility and loving temperament. I remember that a neighbor brought him to our house accusing him of having bitten a child, and along with the man came many neighbors who defended our dog saying that it was not him. After several inquiries and discussions among neighbors, the truth was reached that Buki had not bitten anyone.

What do I mean by this example? That a good reputation accompanied by the truth in any circumstance will free us from any accusation. When I think about our Buki, I remember his innocent face, and it makes me very tender to think of him as someone who was alone and without defense, but who was saved by his good reputation.

There is something great inside you. Even if you are alone, it will emerge and be your defense in moments of harassment. You will find healthy connections with the right people who will push you forward and accompany you on your path to success. Do you know what is great about success? Succeeding after no one believed in you.

SUCCESS IS A PROCESS

CHAPTER 2

Success is the result of opportunities and preparation. Success is not instantaneous, it is not a moment, an event, or a place.

Most people strive to be rich and famous, when according to the Word of God, riches go beyond finances, so we could say that success is a process that includes the comprehensive realization of each area of our life. What an interesting approach, right?

Success is growth and development. It's putting passion into what you do. It is reaching a goal and from there, creating another step to reach a higher goal. We are referring to a trip, a daily and constant work, without fainting.

Most believe that success is discovering the formula to never fail. But it is not true. Success is learning from failure. John Maxwell, a leadership expert, says that failure is the opportunity to start over more intelligently. Failure is only wasted time when we do not learn from it, but when we extract the valuable lessons it gives us, it becomes one more element to build our success. Therefore, we can also ensure that success is perseverance.

Do you know what David's mighty men were like before they met him? **1 Samuel 22:2 (ESV) describes them:** *And everyone who was in distress, and everyone who was in debt, and everyone who was bitter in soul, gathered to him. And he became commander over them. And there were with him about four hundred men.*

David's soldiers had not always been brave. David took a man named Shame and another named Waste and called them mighty soldiers. That was the meaning of the names of two of his soldiers, however, after the process they experienced with David, they became his brave men.

No matter what name you have been given, or what you have experienced, the success that comes from the hand of God depends on total fidelity to Jesus Christ and dependence on the Holy Spirit. That's how compelling and powerful this God's way approach to success is!

Regardless of the name your parents or tormentors have given you, in the eyes of God, you are a brave man of faith. A strong woman of faith. So you must do what God told you, and do it well to be successful.

In the book of the Acts of the Apostles, we see the story of Gamaliel, a Pharisee teacher of the law who advises leaving the apostles free because it was impossible to stop them and prevent the Word from growing since it was evident that God was with them. **Acts 5:39 (ESV) expresses it:** *but if it is of God, you will not be able to overthrow them. You might even be found opposing God.*

If the plans are from God, they will always be successful. That is why, until today, nothing and no one has been able to stop the advancement of the Word of God. If we think about the church, the greatest institution placed by God on earth, we see that historically it has faced every attack and weapon of the enemy, the devil, and always rises powerfully from the ashes.

No one can fight against God and his eternal plans. Furthermore, nothing against God can be successful. Accept this glorious truth and act on it to build your success!

BE UNCONDITIONAL HELP

CHAPTER 3

The Lord tells us that if we wait on Him, we will receive the reward of the inheritance. Think how great God's inheritance is that it supplies everything we need.

> ***Colossians 3:23-24 (ESV) advises:***
> *Whatever you do, work heartily, as for the Lord and not for men, knowing that from the Lord you will receive the inheritance as your reward. You are serving the Lord Christ.*

You know? I happily recognize myself as someone who, from the heart, cares about people. When you help, don't expect to receive something in return; Do everything from the heart as for God, because the day you expect something in return you will feel bitter if you do not receive what you expected.

Who would seek to receive something from a person if we have the promise that it will be God who will reward us? Think that the promise and inheritance of God are much greater and more abundant than any inheritance of men. This divine inheritance covers absolutely all our needs. When you understand this truth, you become a person who gives for the pleasure of giving. That is precisely what we do with my husband; giving has become our habit.

It is so powerful to be generous! My husband, for example, loves giving gifts. That is his way of expressing love and showing that he appreciates the value we have in his life. Those of us who have prayed and worked alongside him for so many years know this. Our effort has had only one objective: to bring people to know God. And it has been wonderful to see that through us God completes the work He began in each life because we allow ourselves to be used by Him.

Ephesians 3:20 (ESV) assures:
Now to him who is able to do far more abundantly than all that we ask or think, according to the power at work within us.

This same verse in The Passion Translation says: *Never doubt God's mighty power to work in you and accomplish all this. He will achieve infinitely more than your greatest request, your most unbelievable dream, and exceed your wildest imagination! He will outdo them all, for his miraculous power constantly energizes you.*

Having a deep spirituality means that all the blessings, resources, and wisdom of God reach us precisely because of that power that acts in us. *For this reason, the Scriptures also command us to be strong in the Lord and in the power of his might…* **(Ephesians 6:10).**

I find this approach extraordinary because it makes our path to success even clearer and easier, as it brings to light our most hidden gifts and talents.

In conclusion, there is nothing better than entrusting our success to God, because only He can do it, and we can achieve it by His power.

SUCCESS IS BUILT WITH WORDS

CHAPTER 4

The Word of God will always produce what it was sent to do. When our thoughts are balanced, good judgment is restored. We can believe the Word, but there is power in confessing it because it has creative power.

I once read: *"It is better to be a seed that God plants than to be a tree that God cuts down."* How true this is!

The words we speak are seeds, they are our hidden potential. When we speak words, we commit to what we say. There is always something nested in our spirit that comes to light when we speak. You can't feel something inside and live with a totally different approach. That inconsistency is lethally dangerous.

> **John 3:6 states:** *That which is born of the flesh is flesh, and that which is born of the Spirit is spirit.*

There will be things in your flesh that will cause you struggles.
Perhaps there are secrets hidden from tragic experiences of the past, but spiritual life does not spring from a carnal seed. Making mistakes has nothing to do with the work that God wants to begin in us. Our Lord is the God of new beginnings.

The kingdom of God is spiritual and only those who have a spiritual life can confess what they know will be fulfilled in them. In my case, every time I speak and preach, I confess with my mouth that I will be a famous writer, and I not only say it, but I believe it with all my being and I work to achieve that goal.

The Word of God lives and remains forever. It is established in the Scriptures, in **1 Peter 1:23 (ESV):** *since you have been born again, not of perishable seed but of imperishable, through the living and abiding word of God.*

So, get ready to release good seeds. We must put aside all the bad things we have experienced, and let go of the past that left old scars that only remained to remind us of our preparation. Yes, everything in life is a preparation to get rid of worries that do not help us move forward, so let them go!
Let go of the past!

The Word of God is effective. But we must align our thoughts with that word and allow it to restore our good judgment. We can believe the Word, although it is not enough, since there is power in also confessing the Word because it becomes life due to the creative power it possesses.

We are conquerors when we take the Word of God for our lives. We can bring joy to the Lord's heart or disappoint Him, but we do not want to sadden Him, so let us believe and declare what He has already said about us. It is time for confession to arise in you, it is time for you to speak to yourself and the whole world: *"I am ready to do what God destined me to do…"* In this way, you will open the doors to a successful future for you and your offspring.

HUMILITY IS NEEDED

CHAPTER 5

Staying humble is one of the greatest virtues that God has given us to help others.

True humility is difficult to understand because of the deception of the human heart. What do I mean? It is difficult for us to recognize that we can improve our dependence on God, even if we see ourselves as good people.

> ***Psalm 138:7-8 (ESV) declares:***
> *Though I walk in the midst of trouble, you preserve my life; you stretch out your hand against the wrath of my enemies, and your right hand delivers me. The Lord will fulfill his purpose for me; your steadfast love, O Lord, endures forever. Do not forsake the work of your hands.*

There is a favor that God gives, that he dispenses, that he delivers to the humble. God rules from the heavens, from above he observes the humble in their anguish, and defends them. Have you thought about it? When we are in trouble, the Lord shows His right hand of power, saves us, and completes the work He began in us because we allow ourselves to be treated by Him.

A young woman from the ministry once wrote me this phrase that I already shared with you: "Remaining humble is one of the greatest virtues that God has given us to help our neighbors." How accurate! Humility allows us to see beyond ourselves and provide our support to those who need it. But humility is more difficult to practice than it seems because it is about shedding our self-centeredness and strengthening our generous attitude.

So, it is important to understand that serving God makes us humble, and that is why God chose us.

Colossians 3:12 (CEV) says it this way: *God loves you and has chosen you as his own special people. So be gentle, kind, humble, meek, and patient.*

It is our responsibility to have empathy for the suffering of others. That's part of the humility that comes with having compassion for someone who is facing loss or failure.
Being humble also implies the inclination to do good, to find a way to lift people out of their condition of poverty, and allow them to raise their standard of living.
Furthermore, it means having the virtue of recognizing our defects and mistakes, being docile and soft, and treating others kindly.

Humility also includes the ability to endure difficulties, annoying and offensive situations without getting angry, on the contrary, facing them as peacemakers. That is why a humble person is successful.

Humble is the one who learns to treasure everything that God gives him, he is the one who values others and respects them, so he does not exercise dominion over his fellow men, as I explain in chapter 23 of my book: *"The greatest frustration of the man: not understanding his wife."*

All of these attributes of humility produce patience to move forward in the process of conquering even what others see as unconquerable. Develop your traits of humility. Remember that only someone humble can recognize that the success of others is also their success.

LOYALTY VS. DISLOYALTY

CHAPTER 6

*Many times our Lord
distances us from
what we think is good
because he wants to
give us the best.*

It is very important to be legitimate and loyal. David refused to kill Saul because he was legitimate; He knew what had happened to Saul for turning away from God and consulting a witch. That's why he said to God: *Purge me with hyssop, and I shall be clean; wash me, and I shall be whiter than snow.* **Psalm 51:7 (ESV).** *Cast me not away from your presence, and take not your Holy Spirit from me.* **Psalm 51:11 (ESV).**

God allows you to see what happens to others so that you do not make the same mistakes. See how interesting? If David had killed Saul, he would have set a precedent for killing kings; It would have practically opened the door for others to kill him.

Every time you fight disloyalty and rebellion, you are directly fighting Satan, who desperately wants to tear down your "spiritual building." The devil knows that if he can tear down the pillars, the entire building will collapse.

Another thing about loyalty is that it opens the doors to what is best for us. Have you thought about how God will feel when his children abandon him?

Luke 15:11-13 (ESV): *And he said, "There was a man who had two sons. And the younger of them said to his father, 'Father, give me the share of property that is coming to me.' And he divided his property between them. Not many days later, the younger son gathered all he had and took a journey into a far country, and there he squandered his property in reckless living.*

It is beautiful to become a parent, but it is also a huge challenge. Like Jacob, you have children in your care with their characteristics and challenges. Our three children are so different, although all three came from my womb, they are mine and my husband's. But that's God, he acts in diversity.

The prodigal son abandoned his father without any protocol, he just left. God experiences this situation when his children abandon him, when they deviate from his ways, and when they are not loyal to the love that he provides. It's tremendous. Right?

It is these children who enter the land of oblivion if they do not repent and return wholeheartedly to the Lord. In that spiritual place, self-confidence is destroyed and self-esteem is completely lost. The Lord told me that that is the place where no one remembers them, there is not even anyone who lifts a prayer for their lives. Be careful!
Warn others about this!

The prodigal son had everything at home. Do you remember what he said in his time of need? He declared that even the servants of his father's house had more than they needed to eat, and he was hungry. He was inspired by demons to go after non-existent fantasies that led him to waste everything by receiving his inheritance early. Every time someone is guided by unclean spirits, they end up in a dark and barren terrain, in the land of oblivion, where disloyalty leads them.

> **The psalmist said in Psalm 88:3-8 (ESV):** *For my soul is full of troubles, and my life draws near to Sheol. I am counted among those who go down to the pit; I am a man who has no strength, like one*

> set loose among the dead, like the slain that lie in the grave, like those whom you remember no more, for they are cut off from your hand. You have put me in the depths of the pit, in the regions dark and deep. Your wrath lies heavy upon me, and you overwhelm me with all your waves. You have caused my companions to shun me; you have made me a horror to them. I am shut in so that I cannot escape.

The devil is the one who takes people to desolate places. The Lord is the one who leads people on the right path to do their best, but we only have access to those blessings thanks to our loyalty.

Psalm 23:4 CEV assures:
I may walk through valleys as dark as death, but I won't be afraid. You are with me, and your shepherd's rod makes me feel safe.

How powerful!

THE SPIRIT OF INDEPENDENCE

CHAPTER 7

Living with open hands and an open heart is a blessing to those around you, and it becomes a reward and success for you.

> ***Hebrews 12:7 (ESV) explains:***
> *It is for discipline that you have to endure. God is treating you as sons. For what son is there whom his father does not discipline?*

In the womb, the baby is connected to its mother. There he receives food, is comfortable, and feels safe hearing his mother's voice. He lives in complete dependence, but it does not last forever, but only nine months. Then, the baby needs to disconnect from his mother. Nature itself teaches us about the need for independence. However, if this baby becomes independent too soon, he will truly die, because he needs breast milk to nourish himself and he needs daily care to grow.

You cannot acquire your independence without giving due honor to your Heavenly Father, since He gave you life. What is the point of living without having a life? Some things may have died in you, but you are not dead. A son who distances himself from his parents, angry and in rebellion, is determining his destruction.

Returning to the story of the prodigal son. A son who despises correction will be destroyed. His parents are dishonored by a son who becomes independent and forgets how much they cared for him and how much they loved him. God allows us to be independent when we must make correct decisions in which we put into practice everything he has taught us. Do not allow yourself to be attracted by the emptiness of temporary successes. The road to success will sometimes be uphill and other times it will be downhill, but our Lord is the God of the mountains and also the God of the valleys, so we must always trust in His guidance and depend on

Him.

Loyalty that translates into trusting dependence will take you very far. Being grateful to our natural parents, even if they have made mistakes, will attract success in everything you undertake. No matter how old you are, no matter if you already have children who call you "mom" or "dad", for your parents you are still a small being who they need to protect. I smile when my mother, to this day, scolds me and calls me "baby".

God understands and loves the baby who still lives inside us. He knows our most intimate needs and is interested in us. What's more, He constantly thinks about each of us, and he thinks well, unlike people. When we understand that we are empowered to fulfill our purpose, we feel healthily independent.

Our Heavenly Father has prepared a banquet in honor of each of us. He gives us the independence we need so that we decide to be loyal and do his will. Let us give thanks for the love of him who is wise and protective at the same time.

PROPHESY LIFE

CHAPTER 8

There are many spiritually dry people who need a word of life. When you give them that exact word, they will accompany you on your path to success.

> ***Ezequiel 37:1-4 (ESV) says:*** *The hand of the Lord was upon me, and he brought me out in the Spirit of the Lord and set me down in the middle of the valley; it was full of bones. And he led me around among them, and behold, there were very many on the surface of the valley, and behold, they were very dry. And he said to me, "Son of man, can these bones live?" And I answered, "O Lord God, you know." Then he said to me, "Prophesy over these bones, and say to them, O dry bones, hear the word of the Lord.*

On one occasion, God gave me this Word and made me see dry bones. Before Ezekiel prophesied to the dry bones, it says that the hand of the Lord was upon him (Ezekiel 37:1). That was why he could prophesy life to them. So you should always seek God to be with you.

These days, the Lord is demanding intimacy, because his hand must be on us to prophesy life. The times that God has allowed me to prophesy under the anointing of the Holy Spirit, those people were marked by the Word; Not only did they change their lives, but today they are the most faithful people who accompany us in the ministry. Perhaps your life has been one of disappointments, betrayals, and misfortunes, so you do not have the strength to prophesy life about anything. But my advice is to never blame God for your pain, but rather thank Him for being a survivor.

There is no lasting success if God is not in the matter. He always has promises that bear your name. A new assignment is on the way. Every day of my life, I ask the

Lord to give me new people on my path to help them and impart abundant life into them. So their success is my success.

The Word of God says in **John 10:10** that Jesus Christ came to give us life and life in abundance. When you understand this, your entire perspective changes. This is the meaning of the word abundance in Strong's Dictionary: *"Superabundance, excessive, overflowing, excess, more than sufficient, profuse, extraordinary, much more than is necessary."*

The Fullness Bible, in **John 10:10,** says: *Jesus said he was coming to give life; not just ordinary existence, but life in fullness, abundance, and prosperity.*

> ***3 John 1:2 (ESV) says:*** *Beloved, I pray that all may go well with you and that you may be in good health, as it goes well with your soul.*

On the one hand, there is God offering goodness, life, and much of everything necessary for life. I recommend you read ***Joel 2:26 and 2 Peter 1:2 (ESV).*** On the other hand, there is the enemy of our soul, who comes to deprive us of the blessings of God, to oppress our body through illness and accidents, to destroy everything we love and cherish.

The first step to experiencing complete biblical prosperity is to believe that it is God's greatest desire for us. The second step is to submit our desires to God. In this way, aligned with the Lord, our words and statements will be powerful to give life and give it in abundance.
Let's speak positively!

STUBBORNNESS VS. WISDOM

CHAPTER 9

The Bible says that in the multitude of counselors there is wisdom. Timely advice is a warning, something that will free you from a bad action.

WITHOUT FEAR OF SUCCESS

> ***Proverbs 15:22 (ESV) teaches:***
> *Without counsel plans fail, but with many advisers they succeed.*

There is nothing better than having a teachable spirit to climb the ladder of success. Foolishness and stubbornness are sisters. A foolish person is generally stubborn and inflexible. He doesn't listen to reason, doesn't listen to advice. In fact, a fool will hate you for giving him sound advice. This is a common characteristic of the spirit of foolishness.

Perhaps several people spoke to the prodigal son regarding his decision to leave. Perhaps his father, mother, uncles, and aunts tried to give him advice, but the spirit of foolishness made the person deaf. Seek to be wise and listen to good advice that will preserve your life.

> ***Colossians 2:3 (ESV) says of Jesus:***
> *in whom are hidden all the treasures of wisdom and knowledge.*

In Jesus Christ and only in Him are hidden wisdom and knowledge that are treasures, those unfathomable treasures that reach the depths of God. They have no bottom and are hidden. Powerful!

I imagine an open mine where highly valuable minerals can be found permanently; by searching hard, it is possible to find precious stones of wisdom. This is Jesus Christ, He is our wisdom.

On the path to success, we need wisdom and understanding. ***Proverbs 3:16*** says that he who finds

wisdom obtains long life is in her right hand; in her left hand are riches and honor. That is, wisdom offers longevity, vitality, joy, and peace.
Dear Lord, thank you!

SHAME OR BRAVERY

CHAPTER 10

It is extraordinary to know that we have a God who goes before us, who fights for us, and who cares for us. I don't know about you, but this truth strengthens me and fills me with courage.

The Apostle Paul said in Romans 1:16 (ESV): *For I am not ashamed of the gospel, for it is the power of God for salvation to everyone who believes...*

How many times has it happened to you that you talk to people at work or in the supermarket, but you don't talk to them about the Gospel? You are the one who brings the good news because the Gospel is "good news," something many people need today! Right? On the path to success with God, we must talk about his work in our lives.

Are you one of those who think that God owes you something?
How many times have you testified how the Lord helped you achieve success? He made us unique, and original and gave us gifts and abilities that cannot be duplicated. He did it so that we would fulfill a purpose and plan determined before the foundation of the world. Imagine that! So from today, do not be ashamed to talk about Christ, so that one day, the Lord will not be ashamed of you before the Father.

Deuteronomy 31:6 (ESV) asks: *Be strong and courageous. Do not fear or be in dread of them, for it is the Lord your God who goes with you. He will not leave you or forsake you.*

I always say, "If God helped us in a situation in the past, He will do it again in the present". That conviction fills me with the courage to face something new every day, sure that I am not alone, and that I have the true, powerful, and omnipotent God by my side.

Think about it, the same thing happens to you. You and I should be grateful for such a privilege.

I read that if we put an eagle in a chicken coop, even if it is the same size as the chickens, the eagle always sees further, because it is not a chicken, it is an eagle. Even if he doesn't know how to fly yet, he already has vision. You are an eagle and God gave you vision; furthermore, he speaks to you in many ways, one of them is through visions.

These are times when we will have a fresh vision. This is a time when God gives us eyes to see the future he has planned for us. The enemy has always tried to prevent us from seeing what lies ahead, so that we disconnect from the vision, that we lose hope and collapse on the battlefield.

Sometimes, we give up in the middle of what seems like a desert, but we are only a few minutes and steps away from conquest and advancement. For our vision to come true we need courage, and to push towards a word of faith. We must not lack faith to overcome shame and grow in courage. Think about it.

POWER...
WHAT FOR?

CHAPTER 11

Success is speaking and proclaiming the truth and the Gospel of Christ. We cannot remain silent about what we have experienced.

> **Acts 1:8 (ESV) explains:**
> But you will receive power when the Holy Spirit has come upon you, and you will be my witnesses in Jerusalem and in all Judea and Samaria, and to the end of the earth.

Nowadays, there is a lot of talk about empowerment. But do believers understand what that means biblically? The disciples believed that Jesus Christ would establish a kingdom for the restoration of Israel, but He came to earth as the Messiah, Savior of souls, as the long-awaited Redeemer. So, for what and why is there so much talk about power?

Foremost, to have power you must receive the Holy Spirit in your life. Not all believers have; if they had, we wouldn't have to remind them to testify because they would do it naturally and spontaneously. When you receive the Holy Spirit, you become a witness. What does a witness do? They speak, they say what they saw and heard.

Additionally, a witness testifies under oath to tell the truth. Those of us who are witnesses, and act with the power that the Lord Jesus Christ gives us, speak and proclaim the Gospel of Christ. That truth that we cannot silence because we have experienced it. When we act as witnesses, what happens? The Holy Spirit confirms our testimony with miracles and supernatural and extraordinary gifts.

The Greek word for "witness" is martyr; for this reason, those who seal their testimony by giving their lives for faith in Jesus are called martyrs. Today, that means investing time to proclaim the Gospel to every creature, as the Word says; without forgetting those who have given everything for the cause of Christ. It is the power of the Gospel that attracts people. Life is the Lord expressed in each of us. And it says in:

Ephesians 6:10 (ESV)
be strong in the Lord and in the strength of his might

Strengthening ourselves in the Lord is knowing that our spiritual strength, our wisdom, and peace come from Him. Think about it, that is true success.

THE HAND OF GOD OVER MY LIFE

CHAPTER 12

Make the Lord smile from where you are, surpassing yourself until achieving all that, by His grace, He expects you to be... You must overcome your challenges."

> ***Isaiah 41:10 (ESV) motivates:*** *fear not, for I am with you; be not dismayed, for I am your God: I will strengthen you, I will help you, I will uphold you with my righteous right hand.*

What can we fear when we hold the hand of God? Each of us enjoys protection that allows us to silence fears and grow in faith. The hand of God directly cares for our lives. Even more, have you realized that he has been taking care of us throughout our existence? That truth is so intense that it cannot be explained, only appreciated because it fills us with security and complete confidence.

Proverbs 3:24-26 (CEV) assures: *you will rest without a worry and sleep soundly. So don't be afraid of sudden disasters or storms that strike those who are evil. You can be sure that the Lord will protect you from harm.*
How powerful! He protects us, He blesses us and He covers us.

Think about it, God loves us so much that he takes care of our rest so that no bad dreams keep us tied to the past. How awesome! He has time and again met our needs and bound up our wounds with his grace. How wonderful!

What a privilege it is to have available the treasures of his infinite grace. ***Joshua 1:8 (ESV)*** *says that the divine plan considers that you will make your way prosperous, and then you will have good success.* We must constantly meditate on the Scriptures because there lie the most powerful secrets, in addition to every moral and spiritual rule, to succeed.

But the most important thing is to put it into practice, to not only be hearers but also doers of the Word.

Overcome your challenges, and move forward, you were born to succeed. How to defeat failure? Striving with faith to succeed in everything you undertake. Do you need anything else? Courage, the Mighty One of Israel is with you!

YOUR HEART'S DESIRE

CHAPTER 13

We are unable to achieve lasting success without the Lord. We need him. Every person who wants to achieve success alone remains lonely.

> ***Psalms 20:1-4 (ESV) gives us hope:*** *May the Lord answer you in the day of trouble! May the name of the God of Jacob protect you! May he send you help from the sanctuary and give you support from Zion! May he remember all your offerings and regard with favor your burnt sacrifices! May he grant you your heart's desire and fulfill all your plans!*

I like this psalm because I think it expresses God's true desire: to bless us. But there is a detail, and that is that the Lord himself will free us in the days when tribulations or conflicts come. We will always have battles! But it is there where we must trust our successes to God since the basis of every relationship is trust.

Problems are inevitable in marriages, families, businesses... in all areas, but the promise is given: when we pray, He will hear us. What's more, God knows we will make a mistake before we even make it. There is nothing that the Father does not know.

So let us seek solitude to meet Him and listen to His voice stripped of all distractions. It is his peace that will bring serenity and strength; It is the hand of Jesus, the Potter, that will rebuild the damaged edges of your life. We cannot achieve lasting success without the Lord, we need Him because we cannot do it alone, and if we try, we will not be alone.

The best favors come from God, from his sanctuary, from where God remembers all our offerings. Those that also speak of sacrifice, of serving in the church, of listening to him and obeying him. In that context, God will give you the desires of your heart.

What things do you want? Be faithful to His Word and your desires will be fulfilled. New cycles of victory, success, and prosperity will replace old cycles of failure, poverty, and death in your life. Hallelujah!

ENJOYING IN THESE TIMES IS DECISIVE

CHAPTER 14

Rejoicing indicates much more than enjoying yourself. It is a feeling of well-being and joy of the heart that is reflected on our countenance."

> ***Habakkuk 3:17-19 teaches:*** *Though the fig tree should not blossom, nor fruit be on the vines, the produce of the olive fail and the fields yield no food, the flock be cut off from the fold and there be no herd in the stalls, yet I will rejoice in the Lord; I will take joy in the God of my salvation. God, the Lord, is my strength; he makes my feet like the deer's; he makes me tread on my high places.*

To rejoice is to be happy. Rejoicing contains the idea of dancing, of jumping for joy, of reflecting the joy of the heart through our countenance and attitudes. Our Lord is a joyful God who rejoices for and with his people. Was Israel at its best when the prophet Habakkuk said these words? No, because the people of Israel had suffered the Babylonian destruction. Success was not on their side.

Although everything was wrong in the world around him, the prophet leaped for joy at his communion with the Lord. He chooses to praise Him because He is a faithful God, even amid devastating circumstances. The people of Israel, God's chosen people, always rose from the ashes. Although they were rebellious and disobedient, God was and is always with them.

We are changeable, inconstant, fragile as a spider web, and weak as a reed, but the joy of the Lord strengthens us. It is not our joy that gives us strength, but the joy of God in us. Looking with the eyes of faith is powerful because we do not see our present, which may not be the best, but we project ourselves into the future. In God is the strength for our life and a sure success. This truth is extraordinary, don't you think?

THE STRONG AND THE WEAK

CHAPTER 15

In any situation, seek God, surrender to his mercy, because only in his hands will you receive true transformation.

> ***1 Corinthian 1:25 (ESV) explains:*** *For the foolishness of God is wiser than men, and the weakness of God is stronger than men.*

People watch what we do more than what we say. Right? Now, there are two kinds of personalities, the strong and the weak. Whoever has a strong personality can command others to do things for them. Another of their characteristics is confidence in what they say or do. They may not be right, but say it with such conviction that they infect others with their ideas. They may come to accept their mistakes, but will never feel guilty of them. They usually take the lead. They walk with their head up. They look straight ahead when they speak, "fix" their eyes on the interlocutor. When they greet you, they shake your hand tightly.

Whether it is a man or a woman, in the family they will be the one who, as the saying goes, "wears the pants." In its positive aspect, the strong is practical and brings benefits to society. In its negative aspect, they can be dangerous, as they easily fall into tyranny, authoritarianism, and aggressiveness.

Whoever has a weak personality is the opposite. They are a dependent person and in need of protection. They doubt themselves, so they need someone to back them up and support their ideas. They are vulnerable and easy to handle. They do not argue because they feel defeated. They may be right but don't know how to express it. They do not tolerate their mistakes and try to go unnoticed.

They talk little and agree with everyone. They speak

softly and no one takes their opinion into account.

Their appearance is withdrawn, crestfallen; their gaze is evasive. When they shake hands when greeting, they do so without strength, like a child. At work they meekly allow themselves to be bossed around and fall into monotony, unable to make decisions that vary their work rhythm. In the family, the weak allow themselves to be dominated by their partner and their children do not respect them. But it turns out that God uses those who have no power or strength without Him.

"The weakness of God is STRONGER than men," says this biblical passage. Are you strong or weak? Or do you have a little of both? In any case, seek the Lord, and surrender to his mercy, since only in his hands will you receive true transformation. Many times we are not satisfied with ourselves, but with God, we receive a new identity, because none of us is the result of an accident. In everything, we will move forward since our life is written by the hand of God.
Strengthen yourself!

ASK FOR JUSTICE

CHAPTER 16

By knowing the Bible verses by heart, which are a defense for every situation in our life, we can ask God for justice.

> ***Psalm 119:17-18 (ESV) asks:*** *Let my plea come before you; deliver me according to your word. My lips will pour forth praise, for you teach me your statutes.*
> *My tongue will sing of your word, for all your commandments are right.*

Can I ask for justice at some point in my life? Yes, by knowing by heart the Bible verses that are a defense for every situation. The imprecatory psalms written by King David **(Psalms 35 and 109)** are God's justice for every situation where others wish our evil. In a word, the Lord takes care of those who wish to harm us. He is our justice. Proclaim along with the psalmist this powerful **"Psalm 119: 93 (ESV):** *I will never forget your precepts, for by them you have given me life"*.

Read the Word diligently, and pray for the understanding that only the Holy Spirit can give you. Go from your knees to the sermon, and from the sermon to your knees. The message does not prosper because it is not watered with prayers and tears, nor is it strengthened with daily meditation. We need more prayer and meditation to understand God's message and His perfect will.

Romans 12:2 (ESV) teaches: *Do not be conformed to this world, but be transformed by the renewal of your mind, that by testing you may discern what is the will of God, what is good and acceptable and perfect.*

When you are outside of God's perfect will, you appear to have His favor, but you are not fulfilling His original purpose for you. It is like those who receive the light in their life but reject it. In this world, there is a small remnant who is faithful and understands the good, acceptable, and perfect will of God. Follow it!

IT WILL BE ESTABLISHED UNTO YOU

CHAPTER 17

Blessed means very happy, fortunate, enjoying complete happiness and of the favor of the Lord.

Psalms 128: 1-2 assures: *Blessed is everyone who fears the Lord, who walks in his ways! You shall eat the fruit of the labor of your hands; you shall be blessed, and it shall be well with you.*

I remember when I worked in the Judiciary Branch and was doing my career there. I was promoted to different positions, and the judge took me into account to promote me to two positions at once. She had been working in that official institution for more than ten years and was very loved by everyone.

Imagine, there were other people with the same possibilities as me, but the judge promoted me because of the way I was and because of the trust she had in me. That is to say, beyond my abilities as an employee, my character and my kindness allowed me to reach the position of Senior Officer. How do you think I felt? Very happy! I said, "I am blessed."

The condition to achieve that state of true happiness is the fear of the Lord. If the parents fear the Lord, the children will also, and the offspring will be blessed. Children must be prepared for life.

This psalm shows us what happens when we put the fear of the Lord into practice.
Let us keep in mind that He is our keeper, that He is for us the Father who never sleeps. He always takes care of each one of us, his children. Those of us who are always willing to move forward are invincible and capable of carrying out each new task because we are constantly moving.

Never think that your best days are behind you; that thought will be your anchor to the past. Take this Word: "It will be established unto you." God tells you, from his mouth this statement that becomes a challenge to seek new opportunities. Take a step forward, and you will see that God moves with you.

SUCCESSFUL CONCLUSION

CHAPTER 18

People can see that the Lord has been with us, that he never abandoned us, and that he has made everything come to a successful conclusion.

> ***1 Chronicles 28:20 (ESV) counsels:***
> *... Be strong and courageous and do it. Do not be afraid and do not be dismayed, for the Lord God, even my God, is with you. He will not leave you or forsake you, until all the work for the service of the house of the Lord is finished.*

How beautiful it is to know that the Lord will not abandon you and will always be with you. It's a very nice promise for these times. Like every promise it has three conditions:

1. Act with energy and vigor.
2. Act with courage and determination in difficult or risky situations.
3. Do not allow yourself to feel afraid.

Then, only then, will you be able to understand that the Lord is with you, and you will be able to enjoy his company, in addition to seeing and experiencing that everything will come to a successful conclusion thanks to Him.

How many times have we had to make decisions that mark a before and after in our lives? Many times! The beautiful thing is that after some time, we realize that God has always been with us and has benefited us so that everything comes to a successful conclusion. Keep forward, do not turn back, for the true God is with you.

My husband wrote these beautiful words that I just shared with you. He is a very, very valuable man in the kingdom of God. Everyone in our family is grateful for his life, for his advice, and for his help. Even our legality as citizens in the United States of America is an achievement that we owe to his sacrifice and the high price he paid, even with his health.

My husband has always led us to more and has motivated us to believe that with God we can achieve everything. For him, it is not acceptable to receive no for an answer, since he drives us to achieve all our goals. My husband is a vital part of the success of the CODM Ministry worldwide. Wonderful and powerful is he as an instrument of God's will!

STAYING ON TOP

CHAPTER 19

If God promised you certain things, you must persist to continue, without listening to the negative voices or recurring thoughts that want to make you retreat."

> ***Isaiah 25:9 (ESV) teaches:*** *It will be said on that day, "Behold, this is our God; we have waited for him, that he might save us. This is the Lord; we have waited for him; let us be glad and rejoice in his salvation."*

There is a popular phrase that says: "The difficult thing is not getting there, the difficult thing is staying". Every undertaking or project will come to fruition if you are persistent. That is why you must be careful what you allow into your life.

Some successes will be born with a lot of suffering. But don't dwell on suffering, because doing so will not allow you to see the fruit of your labor. If God promised you something, he will deliver it, so don't listen to the negative voices that will try to make you back down. I like to remind myself that, even if I am weary or tired on the outside, on the inside I should always be upright, in a good mood, happy, with a shining countenance.

The pain disappears when you have the child in your arms, Right? Those of us who have given birth to a child know this very well. If you find yourself in a problem in your marriage, with your children and in your work, resist and seek the Lord before making a hasty decision. If you are facing financial difficulties, develop new strategies to get ahead. It can be done! If there is an unconfessed sin, seek your restoration. It is necessary to be truly free. And if God tells you NO to something, meditate on his Word, because many benefits will come.

I thank the Lord for the times he has stopped me by telling me, "Don't talk." It has been so powerful to have obeyed him!

It is my trust in his sovereign will that has defeated Satan, who always wants everything illegitimate for our lives. May God save you from difficult situations, and may you ascend to his very arms of love and protection. Knowing that he is always with us, that we have his coverage, and that he does not leave us exposed to the wiles of the enemy is what strengthens us. Victory is always ours when God is with us. Marvelous!

DESPERATE SEEKING PRODUCES UNLIMITED PROTECTION

CHAPTER 20

God's work in our lives has not finished. He still has good and wonderful things to do, to show you, to reveal to you, to motivate you to achieve.

> ***Isaiah 55:6 (ESV) counsels:*** *Seek the Lord while he may be found; call upon him while he is near.*

God gave me this phrase on one occasion when I had to comfort a woman with depression. The Holy Spirit is our present help, our protector, our helper and refuge, our help on the edge of the precipice. God is close, take advantage of that closeness.

> ***Colossians 3:15 (ESV) shares:*** *And let the peace of Christ rule in your hearts, to which indeed you were called in one body. And be thankful.*

We wake up every day thanks to the good Lord: "As long as there is life, there is hope". It is useless to want to hide from our Father, who wants to give you life.
Who else knows us like He does? Say no to sadness, say no to anguish, say no to illness. We can spend our entire lives trying to be healthy, but the first thing is to try to fill ourselves with the abundant life that our Lord offers us, that life that the Word of God speaks of in **John 10:10 (ESV)** *"I came that they may have life and have it abundantly"*.

Let us strengthen our faith, and seek help from our loved ones, then everything will be better. We must move the world with our faith, since believing in the fulfillment of God's promises and striving to achieve them is the key to success and being able to sustain it over the years so that it transcends and positively impacts future generations.

Then, we will leave a powerful inheritance on Earth that will withstand risks and human unrest. Because it

is with the strength that lies in our spirit that we achieve the best triumphs. And by the perfect love of God, we are sustained and driven to win.
Go ahead, keep seeking!

GOD IS ALWAYS WORKING A NEW GENESIS

CHAPTER 21

Even the bad, the Lord turns into a blessing so that we can have a new beginning in every area of our life.

It seems difficult, right? But God is working. It seems impossible, right? But God is working.
Looks like it won't happen, right? But God is working.
It seems like only you feel that way, right? But God is working.
Looks like the sun won't shine, right? But God is working.
Looks like it's all over, right? I tell you and I repeat to you that God is working.
Looks like that dream won't come true, right? Lift your head because God is working.
It seems that the enemy is stronger, right? God is bigger, do you know why? Because He is working in your favor. And the Bible says that: *"Nothing is impossible for God"*.

God is working in your home and your family. Furthermore, always remember that Jesus Christ will return.

> **Genesis 50:20 (ESV):** *As for you, you meant evil against me, but God meant it for good, to bring it about that many people should be kept alive, as they are today.*

God speaks to us about new beginnings, of a new genesis. The enemy always tries to destroy what God wants to do in each life, but He transforms everything for good. That conviction strengthens our faith that has been tested amid difficulties. Our Lord preserves our lives and those we love. Rejoice, rejoice, rejoice in the wise love and support of our Lord.

> **Psalms 5:11 (ESV) encourages:** *But let all who take refuge in you rejoice; let them ever sing for joy; and spread your*

protection over them, that those who love your name may exult in you.

Those of us who truly love God know that within us there is always joy and desire to live that only comes from Him. Strengthen your trust in God, and seek Him with faith so that your peace of mind will depend on Him. Only He has been able to get us out of so many situations, and He will continue to do so if we give our lives to Him. Thank you, Lord, infinitely, thank you!

WHAT WAS LOST

CHAPTER 22

Jesus Christ comes to rescue, not only humanity, but also the kingdom of God in the land.

> ***Matthew 5:3 (CEV) says:*** *God blesses those people who depend only on him. They belong to the kingdom of heaven!*

Some trust in God only because they have no one else to trust. They are humble and simple people who truly depend on the only one who can answer for them: Jesus Christ of Nazareth. What good news it is to know that there are no requirements to receive God's grace and favor because all you need is a simple heart that recognizes your absolute dependence on Him. Are you one of those people? Think about it.

> ***Luke 19:8-10 (ESV) relates:*** *And Zacchaeus stood and said to the Lord, "Behold, Lord, the half of my goods I give to the poor. And if I have defrauded anyone of anything, I restore it fourfold." And Jesus said to him, "Today salvation has come to this house, since he also is a son of Abraham. For the Son of Man came to seek and to save the lost".*

The complete change in Zacchaeus' attitude and the way he recognized his actions when he came face to face with the King and Sovereign God is amazing. The recognition he had of the Lord gave him the possibility of salvation. But most notable are the words of our Lord: For the Son of Man came to seek and to save that which was lost.

What had been lost? Zacchaeus was lost, he entered into the declaration of Jesus Christ. Plus, there was something much bigger that had been lost. The authority, dominion, and power that the Lord gave to

Adam and Eve. They lost the opportunity to be God's representatives or ambassadors on earth. The devil, through temptation, deceived them and took away what belonged to them by right, given by God the Father.

Jesus Christ is the one who rescues and restores what was lost. He is the last Adam, who died and rose again. For there to be resurrection, there must first be death. Then he revives everything dead, by the power of the resurrection that comes from Jesus Christ, our Savior.

TRUE SUCCESS IS BEING A PART OF HIS KINGDOM

CHAPTER 23

Everything you do in favor of your personal earnings, without taking into account the calling of God, is a waste of time. We must be faithful to the eternal calling to serve Him because there lies our success.

God has given the church all authority, dominion, and power. We are His church and He expects us to establish the authority, dominion, and power of His Kingdom on earth, as His children and ambassadors. Why ambassadors? Because an ambassador represents a government with all its authority; they represent the dominance and power of that government and its influence.

So, let us recognize that we must place God in his place, the place of preeminence, as Zacchaeus did, to save what we had lost or that we gave into the hands of the enemy... Seize it, rescue it, take dominion with all the authority and the power of the Kingdom of Heaven. Furthermore, in that Kingdom, there is something we must long for: to serve Him.

Look at this Bible story in **Luke 5:1-11 (CEV):** *Jesus was standing on the shore of Lake Gennesaret, teaching the people as they crowded around him to hear God's message. Near the shore he saw two boats left there by some fishermen who had gone to wash their nets. Jesus got into the boat that belonged to Simon and asked him to row it out a little way from the shore. Then Jesus sat down in the boat to teach the crowd. When Jesus had finished speaking, he told Simon, "Row the boat out into the deep water and let your nets down to catch some fish." "Master," Simon answered, "we have worked hard all night long and have not caught a thing. But if you tell me to, I will let the nets down." They did this and caught so many fish that their nets began ripping apart. Then they signaled for their partners in the other boat to come and help them. The men came, and together they filled the two boats so full that they both began to sink. When Simon Peter saw this happen, he knelt down in front of Jesus and* said, "Lord, don't come near me! I am a sinner." Peter and everyone with him were completely surprised at all the fish they had caught. His partners James and John, the sons of Zebedee, were surprised too. Jesus told Simon, "Don't be afraid! From now on you will bring in people instead of fish." The men pulled their boats up on the shore. Then they left everything and went with Jesus.

Our success lies not in seeking personal gain, but in serving God wholeheartedly. When God called the prophet **Jeremiah 1:5-7 (CEV)** he said to him: "Jeremiah, I am your Creator, and before you were born, I chose you to speak for me to the nations." I replied, "I'm not a good speaker, Lord, and I'm too young." "Don't say you're too young," the Lord answered. "If I tell you to go and speak to someone, then go! And when I tell you what to say, don't leave out a word!"

Let us never tire of talking about the wonders and miracles that the Lord has done in our lives. It doesn't matter how old we are because if we have the Holy Spirit, He will put the right words that we should speak.

PASSION FOR YOUR ETERNAL CALLING

CHAPTER 24

Without God, all human effort is useless. And every human outburst stops payment and reward.

We must always do what the Lord did. **Mark 16:15-18 (ESV)** shares: And he said to them, *"Go into all the world and proclaim the gospel to the whole creation. Whoever believes and is baptized will be saved, but whoever does not believe will be condemned. And these signs will accompany those who believe: in my name they will cast out demons; they will speak in new tongues; they will pick up serpents with their hands; and if they drink any deadly poison, it will not hurt them; they will lay their hands on the sick, and they will recover"*.

If we preach, if we teach the Word of God, miracles will happen and people will believe the truth. There are no miracles if there is no preaching of the Word of God.

> ***Hebrews 4:12 assures:*** *For the word of God is living and active, sharper than any two-edged sword, piercing to the division of soul and of spirit, of joints and of marrow, and discerning the thoughts and intentions of the heart.*

So, when you are passionate about your eternal calling and work for God, you will always see a reward, just as Peter did when he lent the boat to Jesus. He got into one of the boats, which belonged to Simon, and asked him to take it a little further from the shore. Then he sat down and taught the crowd.

Serving our Lord brings retribution, I testify to that. Since I resigned from the Judiciary job, twenty years ago, I have received more earnings than I had when I worked there, even though I had the highest salary due to the years of work in that institution.

I like this verse from **Hebrews 6:10-12 (ESV):** *For God is not unjust so as to overlook your work and the love that you have shown for his name in serving the saints, as you still do. And we desire each one of you to show the same earnestness to have the full assurance of hope until the end, so that you may not be sluggish, but imitators of those who through faith and patience inherit the promises.*

Some people start a business and things don't go as expected, why? Because all human effort is useless without God. Furthermore, every human outburst stops payment and reward. There are so many who are like Peter who make an effort, even work hard, but they do not receive a reward.

All human effort is limited, but God's power is unlimited. Everything you do is determined by the place you give to your calling. The secret to success is to prioritize it, just as Peter did when he left his company in charge of others and answered the eternal calling by becoming a fisher of men. It's a good thing he was obedient! And you, what are you doing to respond to God's calling? Think about it.

WHEN ABUNDANCE EXCEEDS YOU

CHAPTER 25

Give God everything you have, not something, but everything, and you will see Him act in your favor.

There will always be a time in your life when you will have abundant provision from God, when your profits will be very great. That is called grace, mercy, unmerited favor, and kindness of God. He provides for you, and amid your need that financial miracle can arrive, that from one day to the next, prospers your life and that of those around you.

At that moment we must be attentive to the following Word in **Matthew 10:40-42 (ESV)** which assures: *"Whoever receives you receives me, and whoever receives me receives him who sent me. The one who receives a prophet because he is a prophet will receive a prophet's reward, and the one who receives a righteous person because he is a righteous person will receive a righteous person's reward. And whoever gives one of these little ones even a cup of cold water because he is a disciple, truly, I say to you, he will by no means lose his reward."*

It is sad to see such stinginess in someone who received God's blessing and grace to prosper, but who fails when it is time to give. Some were in need at some point, but now having abundance, they do not tithe or offer. Their consecration is half-hearted because by having a business, they forget the God who gave it to them.

Carefully read the following scripture in **James 4:13-17 (CEV):** *You should know better than to say, "Today or tomorrow we will go to the city. We will do business there for a year and make a lot of money!" What do you know about tomorrow? How can you be so sure about your life? It is nothing more than mist that appears for only a little while before it disappears. You should say, "If the Lord lets us live, we will do these things." Yet you are stupid enough to brag, and it is wrong to be so proud. If you don't do what* *you know is right, you have sinned.*

Remember that the attitude towards Jesus determines our future. Sometimes, He will put an amount of money in your mind for you to give to His work, and you must be careful to respond without hesitation. Peter could refuse, or he could make excuses not to lend his boat to Jesus.
Thank God he didn't do it!

Don't negotiate your calling. Then, God will give you a thousand times more, because he says so in his Word. Glory to God! You can set the measure, but God sets the limit, and He is unlimited.

WITHOUT FEAR OF SUCCESS...

-You may be afraid, but even with fear, you must try.
-Success is a journey, it is reaching a goal and from there, creating another step to reach a higher goal.
-Having a deep spirituality makes all the blessings, resources, and wisdom of God reach us.
-Something happens when we confess the Word of God on our path to success because it has creative power.
-Staying humble is one of the greatest virtues that God has given us to help our neighbors.
-It is very important to be legitimate to help others on the path to success. Someone legitimate will be faithful and loyal to you.
-Everyone wants a reward, but the reward is achieved when you have your hands and heart open.
-To advance accompanied on the path to success, we must release words of life, of life in abundance.
-Those who have a teachable spirit and receive enough wisdom to reach the depths of the knowledge and love of God climb the ladder to success.
-There is no lasting success if God is not in the matter.
-It fills us with courage to know that God goes before us.
-You cannot remain silent about the truth that you have experienced. Act with the power that Jesus Christ also gives us involves proclaiming the Gospel of him.
-How to defeat failure? Striving to succeed in

everything you undertake and overcome your challenges.
-We cannot achieve lasting success without the Lord. We need him because we cannot do it alone, and if we try, we will not be alone.
-It is not our joy that gives us strength, but the joy of God in us.
-People observe what we do more than what we say.
-In the face of problems, your defense will be to know by heart the biblical verses that are a powerful weapon for every situation.
-Never think that your best days are behind you; always think that things will go well for you.
-In every decision, think that the Lord has always been with you and has benefited you to reach a successful conclusion.
-Remember that even if you are weary or tired on the outside, on the inside you must always be standing.
-It is with the strength of our spirit that we achieve the best triumphs.
-God will always speak to you about new beginnings. He even turns the negative into a blessing.
-Jesus Christ is the one who rescues and restores what has been lost.
-Recognizing that we must place God in a place of preeminence will bring the authority, dominion, and power of the Kingdom of Heaven.
-Everything you do will be successful if you place your calling where it belongs.
-God will always give you a thousand times more!

You can set a measure, but the limit is set by God, and He is unlimited. There will come a time when success and abundance will surpass you.

FINAL WORDS

Thank you for allowing me to provide you with a little more wisdom so that you understand your purpose and your assignment. From now on, I wish that you can make the most important changes in your life, which must be lasting and eternal.

I cannot conclude without introducing you to Jesus Christ as your personal Savior. Wherever you are, say this prayer:

"Lord Jesus Christ, I ask your forgiveness for all my sins. I confess you as my only and sufficient Savior. I declare with my mouth that Jesus Christ has come in the flesh, for the glory of God. Holy Spirit, fill my life and help me to pray. In the name of Jesus Christ. Amen."

For God so loved the world, that he gave his only Son, that whoever believes in him should not perish but have eternal life. **(John 3:16, ESV).**

May God bless you and keep you, and make his face shine upon you, and give you peace. Shalom.

Dr. Adriana Calabria is the author of successful books such as *"Man's greatest frustration: not understanding his wife"*, and *"Woman's greatest frustration: not understanding her husband"*, and now she gives you this manual so that you can achieve true and lasting success.

International figure and speaker for women and marriages, Adriana Calabria is a minister with a doctorate in Theology and Pastoral Care, of Argentine nationality, raised in the teaching of the Word of God from her childhood.

She has been blessed with a 34-year marriage with her husband, Apostle Osvaldo Díaz. They are parents of three children: Agustín, Damaris, and Daniela. Her family has expanded with her daughter-in-law Sarai, her son-in-law Domenico, as well as her three young grandchildren: Ethan, Liam, Arianna and 2 more grandchildren on the way.

After an extensive judicial career, she answered the calling full-time, moving to the state of North Carolina, United States, to found, together with her husband, Celebración Osvaldo Díaz Ministries (CODM).

This is a worldwide religious organization, with churches in Portugal, the European Union, Honduras, Central America, Cuba, Nigeria-Africa, and Mexico, which was consolidated as a model and platform to later create a Christian University.

Adriana Calabria invests and enjoys her time in two passions:
1. Helping women everywhere in the world achieve their dreams and serve God.
2. Being a mentor, along with her husband, of a lifestyle that is a testimony for marriages and families.

Adriana Calabria

For presentations, conferences, sermons, workshops, and wholesale book purchases, please contact:

Damaris Diaz
919-229-6650

adrianacalabria.com

www.ingramcontent.com/pod-product-compliance
Lightning Source LLC
Chambersburg PA
CBHW060200050426
42446CB00013B/2914